Splish Splash

Written by Tanya Simms   Illustrated by Bob Barner

ScottForesman

A Division of HarperCollins*Publishers*

A turtle sat on a log.

Two frogs came and sat on it.

Three birds came and sat on it.

Four butterflies came
and sat on it.

Five ladybugs came
and sat on it.

Down came a fly.

Splish! Splash!
They all took a bath!